TULLY AT CHRISTMAS

Available in the Tales of Tully series

Tully's Life
This heart-warming story follows the journey of Tully from street dog to much-loved family pet, teaching young readers about the importance of kindness, understanding and hope.

Tully Takes Off!
Tully has arrived in her new home with her new grown-up, but she does not like it one bit! When Tully sees an opportunity to go back to her old life on the streets - the only life she has known up to now - she takes it with both paws. With a search underway, it is up to her new grown-up to work out what Tully needs and help get her safely home.

Tully and the Sad Day
Tully has woken up feeling grey and cloudy inside and she does not know what to do. She cannot help her big feeling because she does not know what it is. As her different feelings begin to work together in the wrong way, it is up to Tully's grown-up to help her to understand what she needs.

Go To Sleep Tully!
It is night time and Tully is tired, but she does not want to go to sleep. Her new grown-up knows that Tully is trying every trick she can to avoid going go to bed! With lots of adventures planned and Tully needing her rest, Tully's grown-up needs to find a way to help Tully learn to not be so worried about bedtime.

Tully and the Midnight Feast
Tully is a newly-adopted dog settling in with her new grown-up. Since her arrival, her snacks have started mysteriously disappearing from the cupboard and appearing under her bed, she seems to have forgotten her manners, and there are days when she just cannot stop eating! Tully and her grown-up need to work together to help Tully with her worries about food.

Tully and the Scary Day
Tully has woken up feeling scared. She isn't really sure why, but today feels like a very scary day, and she just wants to hide. Tully's grown-up is thankfully there to help Tully manage her big feelings and see that the day is not so scary after all.

Don't Touch Tully!
Tully is settling in with her new grown-up. She has learned that the new grown-up is a safe person and she enjoys strokes and cuddles with them. Then Tully starts to meet new people, who want to show her how loved she is. Unfortunately, Tully doesn't feel the same about people she does not know and trust. It is up to Tully's grown-up to find a way to help Tully with her big feelings and to be Tully's voice, when she can't use hers.

Tully and the Tummy Ache
Tully has a tummy ache and it's making her feel quite grumpy. She doesn't want to eat or drink, and she can't get comfortable. Her tummy is sore and it's getting worse! Tully is in a toilet muddle. So, Tully and her grown-up work together to sort the muddle out and help Tully to cure her tummy ache.

Tully's Birthday
It's Tully's birthday, and her grown-up has planned a special day for her, but Tully doesn't feel like celebrating. As the day begins to unfold, so do Tully's big feelings. Tully doesn't know what to do about the big feelings, so she does a bad thing. Luckily, Tully's grown-up is there to help her feel better about herself, and enjoy the rest of her birthday.

Listen, Tully!
Tully does not always like to listen, especially when her grown-up is trying to stop her having fun. Tully decides that instead of listening, she can be in charge. But when things start to go wrong, Tully and her grown-up need to work out how Tully can begin to find listening a little bit easier.

Tully and the Makeover
Tully has been having lots of fun playing in the mud, but now her grown-up says she has to have a bath. Oh dear! Tully is not sure she wants one of those. She is feeling a bit nervous about what is going to happen to her, but Tully's grown-up shows her that there is nothing to worry about. Having a bath is a good thing after all.

Tully and Vera
Tully has moved in with her new grown-up but she is missing her foster carer, Vera. Tully is struggling to understand why she had to leave, and whether it is okay to have big feelings about Vera. It is up to Tully's grown-up to try and help her to understand loss and endings and why, sometimes, they have to happen to make space for new beginnings.

Tully and the Chase
Tully loves to be chased. It gives her a feeling of excitement which starts off as being fun, but one day the excited feeling suddenly and very quickly becomes a feeling which is too big. Instead of feeling excited, Tully starts to feel scared. Tully and her grown-up need to work out how they can play Tully's exciting game without it becoming a bit too much for her, and causing a muddle.

Tully at Christmas
Things are starting to feel a bit different in Tully's house and all around outside. Tully's grown-up looks different, strange lights are appearing everywhere and people have started putting their gardens indoors! Tully is not sure what to make of this thing called Christmas – she just wants everything to stay the same. What can Tully's grown-up do to make Christmas-time a nicer time for both of them?

Tully Goes on Holiday
Tully has gone on a holiday with her grown-up. After a difficult start, things seem to be going well. But when the fairground opens up, with all its flashing lights, loud music and food smells, Tully's big feelings get the better of her, making her want to run. And she does! Tully's grown-up needs to find her in time to show her that holidays can be fun after all.

Tully and the New Rules
Tully likes lots of things about living in a house with her grown-up, but one thing she really doesn't like is all the rules! Tully thinks the rules are all very boring and her grown-up must want to stop her from having fun. One day Tully breaks her least favourite rule, and something bad happens. Tully doesn't know what to do! Can Tully's grown-up get to the bottom of this muddle so it doesn't happen again?

Tully at Christmas

TALES OF TULLY

Jess van der Hoech

Trauma Tools
& Training

The individuals and organisations mentioned in this book are included with their permission, and do not constitute a recommendation or endorsement of the services they provide.
ISBN-13 978-1-06-86917-8-2
Editing by Sarah Ogden
www.jvtraumatools.co.uk

Acknowledgements

As always, to my trusted editor Sarah Ogden for all that you do to make these books come to life. I will never fully know what goes on behind the scenes, but it is a joy to work alongside you on these projects. Thank you.

Thank you to my supervisor Linda Hoggan for your continued support, encouragement, discussion and much-welcomed feedback on this series. I learn so much from you and the knowledge I have gained form our conversations has been invaluable across my practice, the books and now this series. Thank you.

Thank you to Laura Benham, for your support in giving me feedback, the searching questions, your friendship and of course, the countless conversations about dogs, the content of which has become quite useful! Thank you.

To the children and families who I meet in my therapy room, from whom I have learned more about hope and healing than any course could ever teach me. Your input, ideas, questions and answers are so valuable to me and I will be forever grateful. Thank you.

Preface

The *Tales of Tully* series is based on the adoption of an ex street dog from Bosnia who came to live with me in September 2023. Watching her try to settle and adapt from everything she had previously known to fit in with a new way of life began to present a number of ideas as to how to communicate such difficulties that can be experienced, to others who are in the process of adopting or who have adopted children. The aim of the series is to provide an opportunity to explore different situations, circumstances, feelings and experiences, finding new ways of communicating and understanding each other, through the voice of Tully.

Christmas time can be a big occasion in many households. A lot of effort is put into making the house look beautiful with lots of decorations, there are often more visitors, lots of food and drinks, and the most important part for lots of children is the visit from Father Christmas.

But what can all of these things mean for a child who is adopted? For a child who has come from a house where there were lots of parties or alcohol and substance use, visitors with lots of noise and drinks can be a huge trigger. For the child who has been hurt, a stranger visiting the house and potentially coming into their safe bedroom to leave a gift is not to be looked forward to.

The house suddenly changing with lots of stimuli, colourful decorations and glitter can in fact be overwhelming rather than appreciated. I have heard many stories in my therapy room after the big day, where children have sabotaged what was supposed to be a glorious occasion. Why? Because it was all too much.

For children who go to school, as Christmas approaches, the school day becomes more fun-based and less structured. Staff and children are wearing Christmas jumpers on what has become a national celebration day – lots of things are 'off.' Things being 'off' are rarely well-received by the child who has experienced early trauma, however good the intention may seem to be.

Then there is the battle of the brussel sprout at Christmas dinner. For many families this is the most special meal of the year, but for some children, a big plate full of meat and vegetables is something they would not wish on their worst enemy! For a child already overwhelmed, sitting down for dinner could be the tipping point, if they haven't already tipped!

I knew from working in therapy with adopted children what a tricky time of year Christmas can be and so when Tully came to live with us in September 2023, I anticipated that she would not be settled enough for me to change her safe place so visually by Christmas day. For the first time ever, there was no tree and no decorations. I put up only a few cards, spread sporadically around the house; this was the only acknowledgement of the time of year we were in.

Tully is an exceptionally anxious and fearful dog, and even the slightest change she will respond to with increased nervousness and anxiety. The question for me was all about balance – how much I needed a Christmas tree compared to how much I wanted her to feel settled and safe. Her needs won every time!

This is not to say that Christmas should be cancelled; it can be a time that many grown-ups want to celebrate with their child. But it is all about balance. What was the environment the child came from? How has Christmas been celebrated before? How much does the child want to celebrate? What will Christmas dinner be? Can it be everyone's favourite meal instead of the traditional dinner? And if the 'big man' is paying a visit, are there boundaries around that? Will the safe grown-ups be awake to manage this visit? Perhaps presents need to be collected at the front door by a safe grown-up instead of a stranger having free access to the whole house while everyone sleeps.

By Christmas 2024, Tully will have been with me for fifteen months. We may have a small tree, because she is now becoming much more settled, but we will wait and see what her needs are when the time comes. There is no right or wrong way to have big celebrations; every family is different, every child is different, every dog is different!.

How to use this book

First and foremost, ensure that both you and the child are well-regulated and comfortable when you begin to read Tully's story. Make sure you choose a time when you are unlikely to be interrupted. The child may like a soother, a favourite or fidget toy, a drink or something to suck or chew to help them to stay regulated.

If the child is calm, then begins to try and distract or move away from the reading, make a note of what they have just heard in the text. It is very likely that they will have just provided you with some valuable information about something that they cannot tolerate or want to avoid for now.

The questions have been designed not only to explore the internal world of the child, but to help to develop a common language between the child and adult who are using this book together. The child cannot get the answers to the questions incorrect. Their interpretation of the thoughts and feelings Tully is having may provide some very significant information about the child's own thoughts and feelings. The child may want to expand the answers to talk about themselves and may even be able to make comparisons between Tully's feelings and their own.

Tully at Christmas

The days had turned colder and the evenings were getting darker. It made Tully's house feel different. It made her grown-up look different as well. The grown-up was not even dressed the same as before. T-shirts had been replaced with things called jumpers that Tully hadn't seen before, and it made her feel a bit unsettled.

Tully knew that something strange was happening but she did not quite know what it was. From her special place on the sofa, Tully could see into the neighbour's house across the road. She thought that she could see a tree *inside* the neighbour's house! Tully thought that she must be seeing things.

What might Tully be seeing?

When Tully and her grown-up went for a walk that evening, Tully took a closer look. Tully was right! There *was* a tree in the house, and it had lights on it – lights and things that shone and sparkled. Tully was confused.

That evening some friends of the grown-up came round to their house. Tully went and hid, she did not like people coming to the house very much. It gave her big feelings.

What might Tully not have liked about people coming to the house?

When the friends left later on, Tully noticed something in the corner of the room. It was a pile of boxes wrapped in pretty paper. Tully went to have a sniff.

"There's one here for you too Tully," the grown-up said. Tully wanted to open her box now. She did not like there to be boxes that she could not see inside of.

Why might Tully not like boxes she could not see inside of?

The next evening on their walk, Tully noticed some more houses with trees on the inside. There were lots of sparkly lights inside and outside of the houses. It looked pretty but Tully was not sure about it. She had liked the street the way it looked before. Tully heard her grown-up call them Christmas decorations.

That evening, more friends came to their house, bringing more boxes with pretty paper, and once again, Tully went to hide. Tully really wanted to sit with her grown-up but the friends stayed for ages and ages. Tully got a big feeling.

How might Tully feel about the visitors coming to the house?

The next day, Tully woke up late. She had been hiding for a long time because of the visitors, and had gone to bed late. It was even darker and colder than usual when she went for her last toilet trip outside and then her grown-up did not sit with her for very long at bedtime, instead saying it was too late.

How does Tully feel about her grown-up not coming to sit with her?

Tully heard some strange noises coming from the lounge. Her grown-up was busy doing something. When she went to investigate, she was horrified! There, right in the window of the lounge, was a tree. The grown-up had brought a tree into the house and was busy putting sparkly things on it, right in the way of Tully's view out of the window!

How is Tully feeling about the tree being in her house?

Everything was different. The weather was different, the evenings were different, the grown-up looked different, people kept coming in the house, there were boxes wrapped in pretty paper everywhere and Tully did not know what was inside them and now the inside of their house had a tree in it! Tully had a very big feeling. She did not like all these things being different at all.

How might Tully be feeling?

What worries might Tully have when things are different?

Tully sat in her bed and cried. She wanted everything to go back to how it had been before. Tully liked her house and her grown-up the way they were before.

What is it that might make Tully want this?

Tully's grown-up came into the kitchen and sat beside Tully in her bed.

"Oh Tully, I'm so sorry," the grown-up said. "I thought you would love Christmas but I can see how it might be a bit much for you. Lots of things have changed and must feel different for you and I know that things changing gives you big feelings. These things don't change forever though, only for a few weeks."

Does Tully mind now she knows the changes will only be for a few weeks?

"I'll tell you what," the grown-up said, "you can have some of your gifts before Christmas day so there are not too many new things all at once."

Does Tully like this idea?

"I will take this big tree away so our house looks the same and I will make sure that we don't have so many visitors. When the visitors do come, I will make sure that they are gone before your bedtime so that our routines can stay the same."

Is this a good plan?

At last, Christmas day arrived. Tully had some new things as gifts, but as promised, her grown-up made sure that there were not so many things that would give her a big feeling.

Tully heard her grown-up talking about a man called 'Santa' who would come and leave a gift for Tully, but Tully did not want a stranger in the house. Tully's grown-up left a special box outside their front door and Santa left a gift for her in there, so he could still visit but would not come indoors. He left her an enormous meaty bone and Tully was very pleased with it.

Why might Tully not like Santa coming into the house?

Did Tully's grown-up make a good plan for Santa's visit?

At lunchtime, Tully and her grown-up had a delicious meal. Tully heard her grown-up talking about 'Christmas dinner', but they decided that in their house, they would have their favourite foods to eat for lunch. Tully had beef and chicken - delicious!

What would you have for Christmas dinner if you could have your favourite foods?

That evening, Tully and her grown-up sat together on the sofa as they always did. And as the days went by, slowly, the lights and sparkly things in and out of people's houses started to disappear. The trees were no longer in people's houses and the world started to look like it had done before.

Even though some things changed for a little while, Tully was pleased that some things always stay the same.

What things stayed the same for Tully?

What are the things that Tully would most like to stay the same?

What worries might Tully have when things change around her?

What can Tully' s grown-up do to help her with these worries?

About the author

Jess van der Hoech is a qualified therapist who has spent the last ten years studying and working with the impact of developmental trauma and, in particular, the assessment and treatment of children and adolescents with complex trauma and dissociation.

As well as supporting birth families, Jess works with looked-after and adopted children and families, using skills in attachment-focused therapy and therapeutic parenting techniques.

Jess is a supervisor, trainer and motivational speaker with a passion for writing therapeutic books that are accessible to children and families to help with the healing process and to increase awareness in the impact of trauma.

Also by Jess van der Hoech

What A Muddle (2016) ISBN 978 18381987 0 1 (Co-authored with Renée Potgieter Marks)
An interactive, practical workbook designed to help children who have difficulties with emotional regulation to begin to understand what is happening in their bodies. A variety of activities throughout the book enable the child to start to explore these ideas through the story of Sam, while gently encouraging them to begin to verbalise their own experiences. Carrying out the physical exercises in the book can promote changes in emotional regulation. The text is written in a child-friendly, gender-neutral style, and is easy to understand for parents, carers and practitioners alike. For children aged 4-12.

These Three Words (2018) ISBN 978 18381987 5 6
Also available as an e-book. A unique therapeutic novel for teenagers with the aim of linking together the feelings, emotions and behaviours connected to anxiety, with some of the therapeutic tools that can be used in order to enable better self-regulation, increased confidence and different ways of thinking. The book is equally valuable to parents of teenagers with anxiety, giving them an insight and understanding into some of the issues that may be affecting their child, and potentially opening up a line of communication and a way forward between parent and teen.

These Three Words: The Journal (2019) ISBN 978 18381987 2 5
A thought-provoking and hands-on workbook, combining a series of practical exercises and tools designed to assist teenagers who are struggling with the symptoms of anxiety. Addressing the anxious responses in both brain and body, this journal provides the reader with the opportunity to discover therapeutic coping techniques and learn how to apply them to their own personal problem areas, before committing to a twenty-eight-day practice to promote good emotional regulation and reduced anxiety. The journal can be used alongside the therapeutic novel These Three Words, or as a standalone workbook, and it is suitable for use by the teenage reader on their own, with a parent, or in a group.

Beastie, Baby and the Brand-New Mummy (2022) ISBN 978 18381987 3 2 and *Beastie, Baby and the Brand-New Daddy (2022) ISBN 978 18381987 4 9*
A therapeutic story that looks at the external signs of pathological dissociation in a child. Dolly's story helps children who have experienced early trauma to begin to understand, in a very simple way, what dissociation is and why it has happened in their internal world. Tools and techniques are included within the story that parents and caregivers can use to assist the child in the first stages of their healing process. Beautiful illustrations on every page enhance the story of Dolly, and help the reader to relate to the events that happen, to notice the methods Dolly has developed to manage her feelings, and to think about what is happening in their own internal world. For children aged 4-12

Printed in Great Britain
by Amazon

62815444R00025